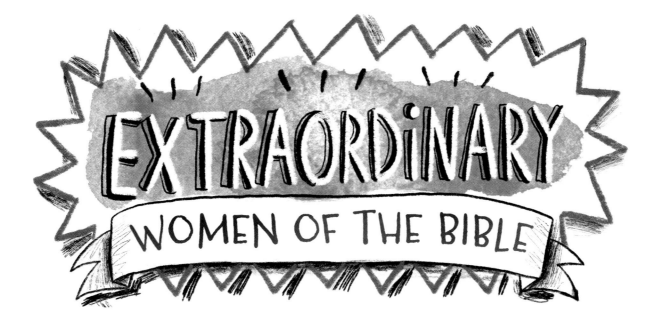

EXTRAORDINARY
WOMEN OF THE BIBLE

For Lizzie and Anna

EXTRAORDINARY
WOMEN OF THE BIBLE

WRITTEN BY
MICHELLE SLOAN

ILLUSTRATED BY
SUMMER MACON

DEBORAH

Deborah was a very wise and courageous woman. She was a judge, prophet, warrior and poet.

Deborah's extraordinary story can be found in the Old Testament, Judges 4—5.

Deborah the Prophet

Deborah was a prophet, which means a special messenger for God. She could explain God's plans to the Israelites.

Hold on a minute, God.

PLEASE WAIT HERE

Deborah the Judge

Sitting under a palm tree, Deborah would use her wisdom to help the people of Israel with their problems and arguments.

NEXT!

Mmm, this can't go on. Something must be done.

Deborah had a message from God. She told a man named Barak to gather an army for battle. Barak was afraid and so Deborah agreed to come too.

Deborah, if you're not going, I'm not going!!!

Deborah the Warrior

At that time, Deborah's people – the Israelites – were very unhappy. The King and his army commander, Sisera, were mean and cruel to the Israelites.

They set off together with their army up to Mount Tabor. There, they watched and waited for Sisera to come.

Sure enough, Sisera arrived with his army at the foot of the mountain.

Let the battle begin! God will help us to defeat Sisera!

Suddenly, God sent a heavy rainstorm, flooding the riverbed. Sisera's army quickly became stuck in the mud! Seeing their chance, Barak and his army charged down the mountain and won the battle.

Deborah the Singer

Deborah liked to sing songs. After the battle at Kishon, she and Barak sang a special song telling the story of their victory.

Hey, wait your turn!

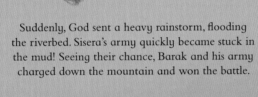

Thanks to Deborah, there was peace across the land for 40 years!

You pushed in! I was here before you!

I will sing, I will play music to Israel's God, the LORD.
I shall march, march on, with strength!
Lead on, Deborah, lead on!
Lead on! Sing a song! Lead on!

Deborah's story reminds us that, with God at our side, we have no reason to feel afraid.

ESTHER

Esther has her own extraordinary book in the Old Testament.

Esther was an orphan and grew up in Persia, raised by her cousin, a man called Mordecai. Esther and Mordecai were Jewish.

Haman was a wicked man, proud and mean. He wanted everyone to bow to him. Mordecai refused and this made Haman very angry. He wanted Mordecai and all the Jewish people to be killed. Mordecai begged Esther to ask the King to stop Haman, but not even the Queen was allowed to visit the King uninvited. She might be killed! But Mordecai warned her that even a Jew living in the palace wasn't safe.

The ruler of Persia at the time was King Ahasuerus. He was very powerful and strict. King Ahasuerus wanted a new queen, so he sent out his right-hand man, Haman, to find the most beautiful women in the land.

Esther was chosen, together with lots of other women, to meet the King. On seeing Esther, the King fell in love. Esther would become his queen.

Mordecai warned Esther not to tell anyone that she was a Jew. She must keep this a secret for now.

I will go to the King. And if I die, I die.

Esther knew it was a risk, but she had to be very brave and strong.

Esther plucked up the courage to visit the King and invite him for dinner. She invited Haman too. Over dinner, she revealed the truth to the King – that Haman wanted to kill all the Jews. She explained that she was a Jew too, so she must die along with her people.

King Ahasuerus was furious with Haman and put a stop to his evil plan. Haman was put to death and Mordecai became the King's new right-hand man.

Esther was a hero! She had saved the Jewish people!

Queen Esther and Mordecai called for this victory to be celebrated by Jews everywhere. This joyous festival of feasting and giving is called Purim and is still enjoyed to this day by the Jewish community around the world.

Like Esther, God wants us to stand up for what is right and he promises to be with us when we do.

MARY Mother of - Jesus

You can find out all about Mary in the New Testament, in the Gospels of Matthew, Luke and John.

Hello, Mary, special favourite of the Lord. Don't be scared! I bring wonderful news!

Mary was a young woman, who lived with her family in the town of Nazareth, in Galilee. She was engaged to a man called Joseph.

In the book of Isaiah, in the Old Testament, there is a prophecy about Mary. A 'prophecy' is when the future is predicted.

One day, something wonderful happened to Mary. An angel, called Gabriel, came to visit her! Mary was amazed, but also scared.

Gabriel told Mary that she was going to have a baby. The baby would be very, very special. He would be the Son of God and he would be called Jesus!

Mary was filled with excitement, although she knew that she would have to be very brave.

Mary then rushed to tell her cousin, Elizabeth. Mary sang a song.

*With all my heart
I praise the Lord . . .
From now on,
all people will say
God has blessed me.*

Mary's journey

Mary and Joseph had to travel to the city of Bethlehem to have their names put in a special register. It was a long journey. When they arrived, it was time for Mary's baby to be born.

The city was so busy that there was nowhere for them to stay. The only place they could find was a stable!

There, surrounded by all the animals, Mary gave birth to her son and they named him Jesus. Mary laid him in a manger, which is a trough for feeding animals, as there was no cot in the stable.

Some shepherds soon came to visit Mary and her baby. They told her that they had seen angels filling the sky, telling them that a special baby had been born. They said that he was the Saviour, Christ the Lord!

Mary treasured their words.

A few days later, three wise men arrived from the east. They had spotted a new star in the sky and knew it was a sign that a special baby had been born. They had followed it all the way to Bethlehem.

The wise men opened up the treasure chests that they had brought with them on their journey. Inside were gifts of gold, frankincense and myrrh. Frankincense and myrrh were highly prized spices.

God loves it when we say 'Yes' to his plans for our lives, just like Mary did.

MARY MAGDALENE

What's in a name?

Lots of girls were named Mary in those days so 'Magdalene' set her apart. But it wasn't her surname. People didn't use surnames the way we do now.

Some people believe that Magdalene came from the name 'Magdala', a fishing town by the Sea of Galilee. So maybe Mary was born in Magdala. Others have a different suggestion. Perhaps Magdalene was her nickname!

Magdala means 'tower' or 'fortress' in Aramaic, the language many people spoke back then. Jesus liked to give nicknames to his followers. He called Simon, 'Peter', which meant 'rock'. And he called the brothers James and John the 'Sons of Thunder'. So, it could have been that Mary was his 'tower' of strength? Maybe she was very tall too!

I wonder what Jesus' nickname for you would be?

Mary's extraordinary story can be found in the New Testament, in the Gospels of Matthew, Mark, Luke and John.

MAGDALA · SEA OF GALILEE

I love spending time with Jesus!

Mary on tour

When Jesus visited towns and cities to spread the good news of the kingdom of God, Mary, together with the 12 disciples, joined him. Other women were there too, including Joanna and Susanna. These women used their own money to look after Jesus and his disciples.

Mary proves her strength

When Jesus died on the cross, Mary was there looking on. It must have been terrible seeing Jesus suffer and die.

In John's Gospel, however, we learn that, when Mary visited the tomb after Jesus' death, the stone had been rolled away and his body was gone! Two angels, dressed in white, spoke to her and, turning round, she saw a man. She thought he was a gardener, but he wasn't a gardener – he was Jesus!

Mary was the **first** to see him risen. She was the **first** to speak to him and hear his voice again. This was a very important moment for Mary.

She quickly ran to tell the other disciples the good news – **Jesus is alive! Jesus has risen!**

Gasp!

I have seen the Lord! He is alive!

Amazing!

Wow!

Great!

WE ♡ U JESUS

Jesus is alive! Jesus has risen!

JESUS on TOUR

God loves it when we're faithful to him and dependable, like Mary.

JeHosheBa

You can find out all about Jehosheba in 2 Kings in the Old Testament. She was the sister of Ahaziah, King of Judah.

Jehosheba's nephew Joash was a descendant of King David. This royal lineage contained some really amazing people. One of Joash's descendants would be Jesus!

When King Ahaziah died, Athaliah, his mother (and Jehosheba's stepmother), decided that she would become queen. Athaliah was wicked and cruel. She was so worried that someone else in the family might try to steal the crown from her that she ordered all her grandchildren and anyone else who might have a claim to the throne to be killed!

Jehosheba knew that she had to do something.

She decided to rescue one of the King's sons, her nephew. He was only one year old and was called Joash.

Just before he was about to be killed, Jehosheba and her husband smuggled Joash and his nurse out of the royal palace and into the temple.

You'll be safe with me, Joash!

The crown belongs to me!

Jehosheba kept her nephew hidden in the temple for six years while wicked Queen Athaliah reigned.

Aunt Jehosheba, can I go out to play?

No, Joash, it's not safe! Your grandmother would have you killed!

When Joash turned seven, Jehosheba and her husband decided that it was time for him to become king. They spoke to the soldiers at the temple and asked them to help. They agreed.

The soldiers and guards lined the temple inside and out, then Joash was brought out of hiding to be crowned King of Judah!

Long live the King! Long live the King!

When Queen Athaliah heard all the noise, she ran to the temple. There she saw the new little king, standing proudly. Everyone was rejoicing.

Treason! Treason!

Thanks to Jehosheba's bravery, Joash was now the rightful King of Judah.

Queen Athaliah was furious. She began to tear at her clothes and shriek angrily, 'Treason! Treason!' but the soldiers arrested her and she was taken away to be killed.

Just like Jehosheba, God wants us to be brave, even when we're in scary situations.

QUEEN

Where exactly was Sheba? Nobody is absolutely sure, but it is thought that Sheba could have been where Yemen is today. Others think that perhaps the Queen of Sheba came from Ethiopia.

The Queen of Sheba heard that King Solomon had great wisdom. She was curious about this and wanted to meet Solomon to ask him some questions. So she set off for Jerusalem with all her camels. It was a long, long journey.

The Queen of Sheba wasn't just fabulously wealthy but also marvellously generous. She took gold, precious stones and spices as gifts for King Solomon.

LET'S GO!

The Queen of Sheba took 120 talents of gold. A 'talent' was a weight used to measure gold and silver.

THANKS.

SHEBA

OF

You can find the extraordinary tale of the Queen of Sheba in the Old Testament, in 1 Kings. Jesus mentioned her too, in the New Testament, in the Gospels of Matthew and Luke.

WOW!! I refused to believe the stories about your wisdom until I came and saw you with my own eyes! But you are even wiser than people say!

Some people believe she asked him to solve some riddles. But the Bible says that Solomon answered everything honestly. There was nothing too difficult for him to explain. The Queen was very impressed by him.

When she felt that she knew everything she needed to know from King Solomon, the Queen of Sheba set off back home.

Her trip to Jerusalem had been a great success!

When she arrived, she had a good look around. She wanted to see what kind of King Solomon was and how he organized his palace.

Today 120 talents weigh over 4 tonnes of gold, or the equivalent of the weight of an elephant!

What Would You Ask King Solomon ?

The Queen of Sheba wasn't afraid to ask for help from others. God likes it when we work together.

Elizabeth

Don't be afraid! I've got great news for you, Elizabeth! You're going to have a baby!

The story of Elizabeth can be found in the New Testament in Luke's Gospel.

Elizabeth was married to a priest called Zechariah. They lived in Hebron, in Judah. They believed in God and led good lives.

More than anything else, Elizabeth wanted a baby, but she was getting on in years now. She and Zechariah had prayed and prayed to God, but no baby came. This made Elizabeth very sad and disappointed.

But, one day, Zechariah was visited by an angel called Gabriel. The angel told him that their prayers had been answered – Elizabeth was going to have a baby!

IT WAS A MIRACLE!

When Elizabeth discovered that she was going to have a baby, she was delighted! She was so grateful to God for answering her prayers.

CONGRATS

During her pregnancy, Elizabeth had a visitor. Her cousin, Mary, came to stay with her – the same Mary who would later become the mother of Jesus.

When Elizabeth heard Mary's voice, something amazing happened – the baby in her tummy leapt for joy!

Mary and Elizabeth knew that their babies were very special and blessed by God.

OOOO! LOOK WHAT TIME IT IS!

YAYYYYY!!

EVERYONE REJOICED!

KICK!

When Elizabeth had her baby, it was a boy. They called him John.

Elizabeth's son grew up to become John the Baptist – a very important prophet, who prepared the way for Jesus.

God *always* listens to our prayers. Like Elizabeth, we must be patient to receive God's blessings.

You can read about Ruth and Naomi in Ruth's own book in the Old Testament.

RUTH and NAOMi

Where you go, I will go. Where you live, I will live. Your people shall be my people.

Ruth and Naomi were family. Ruth had married one of Naomi's sons, but sadly, Naomi's husband and her two sons had died soon after. Poor Naomi! She decided to return to her home town of Bethlehem, but Ruth wouldn't hear of Naomi leaving without her.

Together, Ruth and Naomi returned to Bethlehem.

Ruth and Naomi in Bethlehem

Ruth and Naomi were poor and without food, but Ruth had an idea. As it was harvest time, she would follow behind the farmworkers and pick up from the ground any grains left behind. This was called 'gleaning'.

The farmer was a man called Boaz. He asked his workers who Ruth was.

Who is this woman?

Boaz was a distant relative of Naomi's. He wanted to help Ruth so he was kind to her and made sure she could glean safely. If she was thirsty, she was to help herself from the vessels of water. At mealtimes, Boaz offered her bread. He asked the farmworkers to drop some stalks of barley from their bundles on the path for Ruth to gather.

When Ruth returned home to Naomi, she had a full sack of barley.

She came here from Moab, with Naomi. She asked if she could glean and has been here all morning, without having a rest.

Naomi's plan

Ruth told Naomi all about Boaz and Naomi was pleased. Naomi came up with a plan. As Boaz was a relative, he could be their 'kinsman'. This meant that a relative could marry a widow to look after her.

Naomi suggested that Ruth go to Boaz. Ruth did so and, as Boaz slept, Ruth went to lie at his feet.

When Boaz awoke, he was shocked see Ruth! Ruth asked if he would help them. Boaz agreed; it was his duty and he also thought Ruth was rather wonderful.

The next day, Boaz arranged everything so that he could marry Ruth and he wanted to look after Naomi too.

Boaz and Ruth went on to have a baby – a son called Obed. Naomi was thrilled! She would be Obed's nurse. Naomi didn't feel sad any more as Ruth had given her a new family.

God wants us to be loyal and supportive to others, like Ruth was to Naomi.

Anna, the Prophetess

You can read about Anna in the New Testament, in the Gospel of Luke.

Anna was called a prophet or prophetess, which means that she was a messenger for God. It was unusual then for prophets to be women, which made Anna very special.

Anna was an old lady. She was a widow, which means that her husband had died.

She was Jewish and so devoted to God that she stayed in the temple in Jerusalem day and night.

The temple was a very important part of daily life in Jerusalem. People visited the temple for special festivals, prayers, blessings and to give offerings. Some people would travel to Jerusalem from other cities as pilgrims.

Anna was at the temple to pray and wait.

What was she waiting for?

In the Old Testament, it is written, several times, that a special baby was going to be born. These writings are called 'prophecies'. Anna trusted in the prophecy of God's promise, so she was waiting for the arrival of the Son of God. He was to be called Immanuel. In Hebrew, this means 'God is with us'.

Therefore the Lord himself will give you a sign. Look, the young woman is with child and shall bear a son and shall name him Immanuel.

(Isaiah 7.14)

One day, Anna noticed a young family enter the temple. A mother and father had brought their baby boy to be 'presented'. This was the custom for new babies and their mothers, 40 days after they had been born.

Something about this family caught Anna's attention. This baby was special. Simeon, a wise and very religious old man, spotted the baby Jesus too. He approached Mary and Joseph.

He's here! Our prayers have been answered!

Anna hurried over to see what was happening. Simeon immediately recognized the baby as the son of God. This was what they had been waiting and praying for! Simeon held the baby and blessed him.

Mary and Joseph were amazed.

Anna was overwhelmed with joy and praised God. She then told everyone in the temple the good news!

Never give up hope. Be patient like Anna and believe in God's promises.

RAHAB

You can read all about Rahab in the Old Testament, in the book of Joshua.

Rahab lived in the city of Jericho. She was an innkeeper and her house was built into the city walls. Her inn was always very busy as lots of people travelled through Jericho.

One day, two Israelite spies on a secret mission came to stay at Rahab's inn. The Israelites believed that God had promised them this land so they wanted to see the city of Jericho for themselves.

The spies stayed with Rahab at her inn, but the King of Jericho found out! In the middle of the night, he sent his guards to search the house. Quick-thinking Rahab hid the two men on her roof.

Ready or not, here I come!

You can't catch me!

We demand you open the door, Rahab! The men in your house are spies!

There were two men staying here, but now they've gone! They left at sunset, but if you hurry, you'll catch them up!

The guards believed Rahab, so they set off, thinking that they were chasing after the spies.

After they'd gone, Rahab ran up to the roof and spoke to the two spies. She told them that she knew who they were. She pleaded with them and got them to promise that, when they came back with their people, the Israelites, to take the city of Jericho, they would not kill her and her family.

As Rahab had helped them hide from the guards, the spies agreed. They told her that she must tie a crimson red cord to her window and keep her family safe inside as then the Israelites would know which household to spare.

Rahab helped the men climb down the walls of her house and they left the city of Jericho. Once they'd escaped safely, she tied a red cord to the window. **Then, she waited.**

Sure enough, some days later, the Israelites returned to capture the city of Jericho.

'Spare only Rahab and her family!' shouted Joshua. 'Look for the house with the red cord tied to the window!'

Rahab made a wise decision for her family in helping the Israelite spies. She went on to become a distant ancestor of Jesus.

God blesses us when we look out and care for others like Rahab did.

Lydia

Lydia of Thyatira

'The woman of purple'
For all your purple cloth needs.
Christian

In those days, purple was very hard to make! It was known as 'Tyrian purple' and the dye was made from crushed sea snails.

You can read about Lydia in the book of Acts in the New Testament.

Lydia came from a town called **Thyatira** and was a very popular seller of purple cloth. This cloth was used for clothes and for decorating your house and would have been very, very expensive.

Cloth dyed Tyrian purple was not all the same shade, but what made it special was that it didn't fade in the sunlight. In fact, the colour became brighter. The most prized and costly colour was a rich, dark purple.

The cloth was very popular with royalty.

It took thousands and thousands of snails to make enough dye for the smallest piece of fabric. So purple clothes were only for the very rich.

One day, Lydia was with a group of women by the river in a city called Philippi in Macedonia.

Here, she met **Paul** – one of the apostles spreading the word of Jesus, and his companion, **Silas**.

Lydia listened carefully to what Paul had to say about Jesus and something amazing happened. Through hearing these words, God opened her heart.

She realized that she wanted to become a Christian too! She asked Paul to baptize her and her whole family right there and then in the river. Now Lydia and her people were members of Christ's family.

Lydia was very welcoming to her new friends Paul and Silas and invited them both to come and stay at her house for as long as they wanted!

Come and stay at my house!

What is a baptism?
It is a way to show everyone that you are a follower of Christ. It's a special ceremony in which water is used to cleanse and prepare you for your new life with Jesus.

It is thought that Lydia was the first European woman to become a Christian. Perhaps she spread the good news of Jesus to the people who came to buy her very popular purple cloth!

Just like Lydia, it's important, even when we are very busy, to make time for Jesus.

Jochebed, Miriam & Pharaoh's Daughter

The story of these extraordinary women can be found in the Old Testament in the book of Exodus.

TOO HAIRY!

TOO SMELLY!

Jochebed, an Israelite mother, was afraid. The Pharaoh of Egypt had ordered that all Israelite baby boys were to be killed! He was worried that the Israelites were trying to take over, so he sent his soldiers from house to house, listening for the cries of babies.

Jochebed was desperate to protect her baby boy. What could she do? It was getting too difficult to keep him a secret.

Jochebed came up with a plan to hide him. She made a basket out of papyrus reeds and painted it with sticky tar to make it waterproof.

Then, she laid her baby in the basket, and hid it in the tall reeds that grow along the edge of the river Nile.

TOO BIG!

TOO OBVIOUS!

AH-HA!!

HOW TO BUILD A BASKET

INCLUDES:
- WATERPROOF BASKETS
- DECORATIVE BASKETS
- GIFT BASKETS
- BABY BASKETS

NEW BONUS SECTION:
BUILD A BASKET FOR YOUR PET!

Pharaoh had a daughter and the princess liked to bathe in the river. One day, she came to the river's edge and spotted the basket floating by. She was astonished to see a baby inside! Miriam, the baby's big sister, watched the princess pull her brother out of the water.

Miriam knew she had to be brave and speak out

WILL HE BE OK?

OH MY! A BABY!

Miriam suggested to the princess that she could find a nurse for the baby – an Israelite woman, perhaps, to feed and look after him. The princess agreed. Miriam ran home and found her mother. She told her that her baby brother was safe and she was to become his nurse!

Jochebed was astonished. Could this be true? It was a miracle!

From that day on, the boy was cared for by his very own mother and protected by the Pharaoh's daughter until he was old enough to live at the palace. There, he was raised as a royal prince.

The princess named the boy Moses, which is Hebrew for 'to draw out' of the water.

Jochebed trusted in God to save her baby boy.

Don't be afraid! Just like Jochebed, we can trust in God to keep each and every one of us safe.

PRISCA

Prisca was also known as Priscilla. This was a special name for her – like a pet name!

You will find Prisca in the New Testament. She and her husband, Aquila, are mentioned in Romans, 1 Corinthians and 2 Timothy.

Prisca was a tentmaker. Tents were used by people who travelled and moved from place to place. Prisca worked with her husband, Aquila. It was unusual then for women to work with men as equals.

Prisca must have been very good at her job. Often tents were brought to be patched if they were damaged. Prisca and Aquila probably made other things out of leather too, like bags and belts.

Prisca and her husband were Jewish, but had become Christians. They had come from Rome to a place called Corinth in ancient Greece. There they became good friends with Paul, one of Jesus' apostles. The apostles were followers of Jesus who taught his message. Paul was a tentmaker too and they all worked together.

They're mates with Paul!

He's bad news.

Not everyone agreed with what Paul said about Jesus and some people became angry. Prisca, Aquila and Paul had to be very brave.

Tents were made from woven goat's hair and leather. Poles and cord held them in place.

Prisca and Aquila decided to join Paul on one of his journeys as a missionary. A 'missionary' is someone who travels around from place to place, teaching others about Jesus. In those days, this was the only way to spread important information. A woman serving God alongside her husband in this way was also highly unusual at the time.

Prisca and Aquila set off with Paul.

Tentmaking was a perfect job for missionaries as all you needed was a couple of needles and some knives. So they could work wherever they went.

CHURCH MEETING HERE @ 7.00

Prisca and Aquila invited people into their home for meetings to talk about Jesus. So it is in fact thought that they helped to set up the very first churches!

God wants us to be loyal friends, like Prisca was to Paul, and to work together to share God's message.

First published in Great Britain in 2020

Society for Promoting Christian Knowledge
36 Causton Street
London SW1P 4ST
www.spckpublishing.co.uk

British Library Cataloguing-in-Publication Data
A catalogue record for this book is available from the British Library

ISBN 978–0–281–08123–3

1 3 5 7 9 10 8 6 4 2

Typeset and designed by Amy Cooper
Printed by Imago

Produced on paper from sustainable forests